Birgit van Damsen

Hacking Out Safely

Safety tips for horse and rider

CADMOS
EQUESTRIAN

Contents

Acknowledgements

Grateful thanks to Jane Spencer, Jane Brudenall, and Mr Robin Garrett and Caroline Garrett for their kind help with photography.

Imprint

Copyright of original edition © 2002 by Cadmos Verlag
This edition © 2004 by Cadmos Equestrian
Translated by Claire Williams
Project management by Editmaster Co Ltd
Design and composition: Ravenstein Brain Pool,
Photographs: Andrew Baskott, Birgit van Damsen,
Kit Houghton
Printed by Grindeldruck, Hamburg
All rights reserved. Copying or storage in electronic
media is permitted only with the prior written
agreement of the publisher.
Printed in Germany

ISBN 3-86127-944-4

good condition and should conform to the latest standards, where they exist. Only then is it possible to avoid serious accident caused by faulty or out of date equipment.

Correct clothing and safety wear

In addition to wearing riding boots, jodhpur boots or riding trainers with a heel worn with half or full chaps, you should never ride without appropriate protective headgear. Serious head injuries are the commonest form of riding injury and many of these injuries could have been avoided if a correctly fitted riding hat had been

A frayed rein can have fatal consequences.

A correctly fitted hat will protect against serious head injuries.

The Correct Equipment for Horse and Rider

Correctly fitted equipment is a prerequisite for safe and stress-free hacking. Comfortable clothing and appropriate tack, including a correctly fitted saddle, will reduce the likelihood of incorrect aids being given, or even of the horse misunderstanding a correct aid. Either of these circumstances could result in the horse reacting unexpectedly or dangerously, so it is important to reduce the chance of this happening from the start. All equipment should be in

worn. Modern riding hats consist of a hard outer shell containing shock-absorbing foam, a flexible or detachable peak and a three-point harness with an easy to fasten clip.

Always ensure that your hat meets the current standards – at least EN1384, PAS 015 or ASTMF1163. Additional marks such as the Kitemark or SEI badge show that the manufacturer's hats are retested on a regular basis ensuring ongoing quality. Chin cups are now not allowed in the current standards, as tests showed that they could cause dislocation of the lower jaw. It is vital that a hat should fit correctly to the shape of the rider's head. Many retailers are trained to fit hats and can advise on the latest standards so it is worthwhile finding one that can offer this service. A hat should fit snugly and should always be put on from front to back. The back ties or straps should be correctly adjusted to ensure that the hat does not slip forward once done up correctly. Some helmets have ventilation holes to help air circulation.

It is wise to wear a body protector when out hacking, whether jumping or not. Body protectors will reduce the seriousness of injuries to the upper body by absorbing the impact of falls onto the ground or against hard objects, or of any kick. Whilst originally designed for event riders going cross country, now they are increasingly becoming compulsory for many other activities including riding clubs, hunter trials and BHS exams. The garment consists of (often removable) flexible, shock-absorbing foam panels inside a textile covering. The foam is heat sensitive so will mould to the body's shape when warm, and the garment is adjustable by Velcro and clip fasteners on the shoulders and

A body protector will reduce the impact of a fall.

waist. There are two styles of protectors: the zip-fronted and the "tabard", which is put on over the head and fastened around the waist at the front. As with hats, it is vital that the body protector be fitted correctly, as it needs to allow freedom of movement but mustn't move when worn. The current standard is the BETA 2000 (incorporating the EN13158), which also demands annual retesting from all companies bearing the BETA Standard. The standard offers three levels of protection; however, the highest, level 3, is the correct level for all riding.

Riding gloves should also be worn for hacking. These may be made out of soft leather with ventilation holes, or from other breathable materials with reinforcement on the fingers and palm. Gloves will help you keep a grip on the

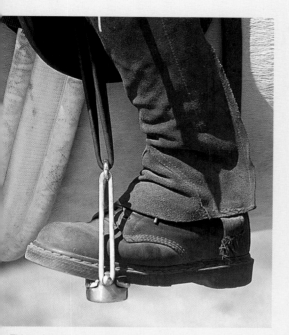

This safety stirrup opens at the side in an emergency.

Western saddles also have their own form of enclosed stirrups, known as a tapedero, usually made from strong leather and attached to the western stirrup.

Safe tack

All equipment used on horses should always be kept in good condition and should be regularly checked for wear and tear. Damaged or faulty parts must either be repaired by a suitably qualified saddler, or replaced. This particularly applies to important items such as reins, girths, stirrup leathers and girth straps. Any leather tack should be regularly cleaned with saddle soap and conditioned as recommended. Conditioning with any of the wide range of leather preparations available will keep leather soft and flexible and will prevent breakages and tears.

reins and protect against blisters, rubbing or friction burns in the case of a fall.

Finally, another important piece of equipment which you should consider for riding out is safety stirrups. These will prevent the foot being trapped in the stirrup and avoid any risk of the rider being dragged. A selection of types are available on the market, all working slightly differently – they may have movable joints, side-opening mechanisms or shaped sides, while others have a system that disconnects the whole stirrup from the leathers in the case of a fall.

Stirrups that are enclosed at the front prevent the rider's foot slipping through and also offer a wide and comfortable tread for the foot, meaning that the foot will not slip out as easily if things get critical. This may help avoid unnecessary falls. There are several types of enclosed stirrups, both metal and hard plastic.

Regular cleaning keeps equipment in good condition.

A running martingale fits to both reins, around the horse's neck and at the girth.

Regardless of what type of saddle is used – general purpose, specialised trekking or endurance or western – all saddles must be fitted to both the horse and rider. For horses with little or no wither it may be necessary to use a crupper to prevent the saddle slipping forward, especially when going up and down hill. A breastplate fitted around the chest and attached to the saddle dees and girth also stops the saddle from sliding back when going up hill.

The bridle must sit flat against the head and should neither press nor rub in any place. The horse should accept the bridle and the rider should be experienced in the use of all equipment used on the horse. Artificial aids such as a standing martingale, side reins or similar should not be used when out hacking since they don't solve any problems and in tricky situations can do more harm than good. If necessary a correctly fitted running martingale can be used as it can stop the horse throwing his head up, hurting both himself and his rider. It can also reduce the effect of a rider taking a tighter hold of the reins than usual.

Safety accessories

There are other useful pieces of equipment that belong to the range of accessories that can contribute to safe riding for horse and rider when out hacking. There is a wide range of boots and wraps that offer protection to a horse's vulnerable legs. These can be made out of leather, synthetic, nylon or neoprene, and offer protection against knocks and scrapes to the lower leg – particularly on and around the cannon bone, fetlock and pastern.

On deep or slippery footing, or when snow or ice makes conditions difficult, studs that are screwed either directly into the horseshoe or fixed to hoof boots can prove useful. They can improve a horse's footing and prevent any dangerous slipping or sliding of the horse's hooves.

In the case of shod horses, so-called hoof grips can help in the winter months against snow build-up. As snow builds up under traditional metal shoes, the horse can end up walking on snow stilts and risks sliding or even slipping over. Protection against snow build-

A saddlebag is ideal for carrying the necessities for longer rides.

Studs like this can prevent a horse slipping on icy or slippery ground.

up involves inserting a thin horseshoe shaped rubber piece between the hoof and the shoe.

If you are planning a longer ride, for example over one or more full days, then it is recommended that the bridle be put on over a head collar, to make tying up during rest stops easier. A lead rope can be tied around the horse's neck and also serves the rider as a neck strap to hang on to when riding up steep slopes or when things get a bit lively.

For the storage of provisions, a first aid kit, rain wear, pocket knife and other necessities, there is a wide range of saddle bags available that are made from an equally wide variety of waterproof and lightweight materials in all sizes, that can be attached to the saddle in different ways.

A mobile phone has also now become one of the necessities of life and should always be

Training to hack out

The best way to prevent accidents is a solid foundation of training for horse and rider, as well as extra preparation for riding out. Many exercises that mirror what can happen out hacking can be practised at home in a safe enclosed environment. Since not every accident can be avoided, every rider needs to know how to cope if the worst happens.

Even in the most isolated of locations you should be able to reach the emergency services with a mobile phone.

Coping with difficult conditions

Uneven or rough ground demands greater attentiveness from the horse as well as sure-footedness. This can be taught through pole work. To do this several poles are laid in a row on the ground for the horse to walk and then trot over. The distance between the poles in walk is between 80 and 100cm (32 – 39 inches) and in trot 135 – 150 cm (3 – 5 feet). The rider should rise to the trot to allow the horse to stretch down.

carried when riding away from home as the best way to reach help in an emergency. Even when you are out of range of normal reception the emergency numbers should still work. Other essential numbers such as vet, the yard and home should be saved on the phone, for ease of use in an emergency when you may be too distressed or shocked to remember them.

For inexperienced horses, narrow paths or bottlenecks can often pose problems. This is due to the horse's angle of vision which, thanks to the position of his eyes on the side of his head, provides a 270° view. Either a horse will refuse to go through a narrow gap, or as a result of fear he will rush through – in itself dangerous if the horse or rider gets hung up or caught on anything. Man-made bottle-necks or narrow paths can be simulated at home

exercise can be repeated with someone in the saddle.

Getting used to dull, hollow sounds such as those heard when crossing a wooden bridge, can be practised by riding over wide strong planks. A horse also needs to get used to unstable or moving footing such as footbridges or ramps, created by placing boards over several car tyres or over a log. Creating such a see-saw over which a horse can be led and then ridden is also good preparation for loading.

Some riders may have access to man-made banks or natural ridge and furrow on which to

Reining back between poles prepares a horse for riding through narrow gaps and possibly getting himself out of danger.

By riding over plastic sheeting a horse gets used to unusual terrain. The alleyway formed by the bales imitates a bottleneck.

using poles, drums or straw bales. The horse can learn to go through the obstacles quietly and calmly, and learn to stand and back up within the obstacles without fear.

Variable footing can also upset an inexperienced horse, especially when it hears strange noises at the same time as setting foot on a different surface. By laying plastic sheeting or old carpet on the ground, anchored down by poles or bales, horses can get accustomed to different footing. The horse should first be led over the reflective and crackly surface until he can walk over calmly without rushing. Once the horse has built up enough confidence the same

*Walking over a seesaw is a good exercise
to simulate unstable surfaces.*

practise riding over uneven ground and up and down slopes. Similarly man-made water obstacles help to get a horse used to more natural water such as streams or puddles. Only once a horse will allow itself to be led through water should he be ridden through.

Finally you should also train your horse to jump over small natural obstacles such as tree trunks, using poles or bales to practise. The horse should be taught to approach any obstacles correctly, and jump cleanly and smoothly. The rider needs to give the correct aids to achieve this. In a working canter the horse should be collected up shortly before the jump to get his attention – only by doing this will he find the correct take off stride. Over the jump the rider needs to put his upper body forward and give enough rein so that the horse can stretch out and balance himself over the jump. After the jump the rider should take up the reins again immediately and canter quietly on.

First aid for horse and rider

More than most, riders who hack out or go cross country need to know what to do in cases of accident or emergency. First aid covers all measures and treatment until the arrival of a

sary cleared (for example in the case of the tongue having been swallowed). The head should be tipped back and artificial respiration given immediately. Heavily bleeding wounds should have a pressure bandage applied to stop the bleeding, using a wad of bandages placed over a sterile dressing on the wound and tied with a gauze bandage.

In the case of arm or leg fractures, clothing should be removed or cut free and the broken joint stabilised using a stick or similar as a splint. The space between the emergency splint and the limb should be padded with clothing or cotton wool. The patient should only be held or touched above the fracture. If there appears to be injury to the spine or pelvis, leave the patient

Jumping small obstacles should be part of the basic training for any horse being hacked out.

Not all riding accidents are without consequences.

doctor or vet, and is aimed at relieving pain and reducing the risk of additional or resulting harm or damage. All responsible riders should complete a first aid course. To learn about emergency procedures in the case of injury to your horse you can prepare by reading some of the wide range of books on the subject or by attending any available courses. All first aid procedures should be practised regularly. In addition it is highly advisable to take out third party or accident insurance.

Injured or unconscious riders should be placed in the recovery position and protected from the elements. If their breathing has stopped, the airways should be checked and if neces-

lying flat on hard ground. In the case of a hard fall you may also have to reckon with internal injuries. In the case of chest injuries the upper body should be elevated, with stomach injuries the patient should be laid flat with legs pulled up to the chest. If the head is also injured in the accident, concussion may result. The symptoms of concussion include vomiting, dizziness and headaches. Bleeding from the nose, mouth or ears indicated a possible fractured skull, in which case the rider should not be moved. The head should be turned to the side to lessen the risk of choking from vomiting. If shock sets in, the legs should be raised and the patient should be kept warm.

Badly injured horses that are lying down should not be forced to stand up, but instead should be calmed by someone they know. In the case of obvious circulatory problems such as shivering or swaying they should be rugged up and kept warm. Bach rescue remedy can be given on a piece of bread to reduce fear and the effects of shock. You should check the required dose of the drops, which are available at most chemists, well in advance of needing them. If the horse is bleeding, it should not be moved. Place a sterile dressing on the wound and put plenty of gamgee on top, fixing this in place with an elastic bandage.

Emergency Procedures

- Stay calm and maintain an overview of the situation
- Catch any loose horses and if necessary tie them up
- Establish exactly what has happened and if required call for help
- Apply any necessary first aid

What to use as substitute bandages:
- Paper handkerchiefs as a wound covering
- Clothing such as shirt sleeves torn into strips as ties or bandages
- Thick clothing such as pullovers, moss or foliage as temporary padding
- Belts or stirrup leathers to use when applying a tourniquet
- Jackets or coats as blankets to keep the patient warm

In the case of arterial bleeding, which is seen by the bright red blood pulsing out of the wound, a pressure bandage should be placed on the artery. If necessary and possible the bleeding should be temporarily stopped by applying a tourniquet on the side going towards the heart, until a bandage can be applied. Under no circumstances should the tourniquet be applied for longer than ten minutes at a time.

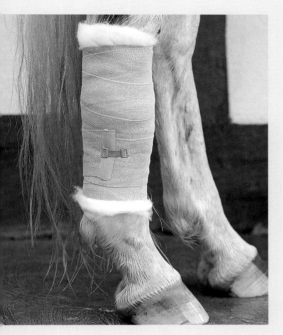

Every rider should be able to apply an emergency dressing.

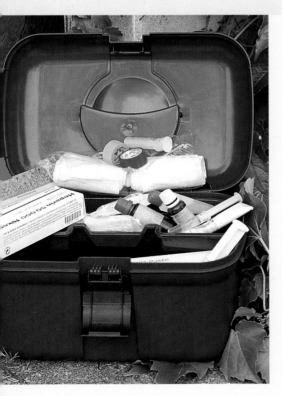

An emergency first aid kit should include sterile dressings, self-adhesive bandages, tape and scissors.

Loading and ride and lead practice

Lame horses, or horses that are bleeding from wounds, suffering from shock or circulatory problems, must be transported from the accident site back to home or to a veterinary clinic. Horses that only load with great difficulty or not at all create more problems in cases of emergency. For this reason a horse must be trained to load so that valuable time is not lost when time is in short supply. Horses that are reluctant travellers may find it easier if they are loaded with a companion. Instead of leading or riding a horse to new grazing, transport it there so that he associates travelling in a trailer with something positive. In the case of obstinate loaders it may be necessary to resort to specialised training or help from an expert who is experienced in dealing with difficult horses.

Riders who hack out should also be able to get an injured rider's horse safely back home. To do this it is useful to learn to ride and lead another. This should be practised at home first. The ridden horse should be 100% reliable and should be able to be ridden with the reins in one hand. The horse being led should be tacked up with his normal bridle or with a head collar and lead rope. Both horses should get on with each other well. The horse being led should learn to walk alongside the ridden horse in a position level with his shoulder without jostling or dawdling. The led horse should also respond to voice commands and signals so that he walks on, trots, slows down, turns and halts

Always practise loading a horse in case of an emergency.

Practise riding and leading at home first...

together with the ridden horse. He also needs to learn to go behind the lead horse when the path narrows. Only when these exercises can be done without any problems at home should you try out the exercise away from home.

In emergency situations you will need to assess whether the horses are likely to bite or kick. If they won't tolerate each other, or if one horse tends to shy or take off, then it is too dangerous to risk. In this case you should call for

...before you try it away from home.

Mastering dangerous situations out hacking

Many riding accidents occur as a result of a lack of foresight or through falsely assessing potentially dangerous situations. The risk of accidents can be reduced if you can identify potential sources of danger in time, follow correct procedures and in certain cases take preventive action. Bad footing, difficult obstacles, precarious situations, bad weather and poor visibility all demand increased caution and attention from riders.

In addition always, wherever possible, ride with at least one other person so that should an accident occur, there is always someone to help.

Obstacles and poor footing

When out hacking, riders will often meet obstacles such as ditches, fallen trees or barriers that block bridleways and these must be either ridden around or jumped over. Narrow ditches and tree trunks can be ridden over by experienced riders and horses in walk, or jumped over so long as the footing allows. Wooden or metal barriers should never be jumped because the danger of sustaining injury over what could be a relatively high and solid obstacle is much too great. Such barriers should always be ridden around, leaving plenty of room between horses.

help and ask someone else to lead or ride the riderless horse home. Providing it is not too risky (i.e. there are no road crossings or other potential dangers), it is possible to lead both horses home on foot at a walk, one to the left, the other on the right. Leading two horses can also be practised at home.

Barriers like this should be carefully ridden round.

The best way to attack wide ditches is to ride obliquely down into the ditches across the slope, when the banks are gently sloped. In the case of steeply sloped banks these should be ridden straight down and up. Always ride in walk, to avoid the horse slipping. If it looks too risky to ride through a ditch you will have to ride until you come to a safe crossing.

Narrow and often overgrown paths will often lead to a dead end. In this case it will be necessary to back the horse up until there is room for him to turn around. If the horse is prepared for something like this it will cope with it without panicking. Always ride narrow paths calmly and at a walk.

You should in principle always ride at a walk when conditions underfoot are less than ideal,

for example, when the ground is stony or frozen, on asphalt, on deep or slippery surfaces as well as on very uneven ground.

When ascending a steep slope it is also best to ride in walk, to avoid a fall by either horse or rider. Riding uphill requires the rider to tip the upper body forwards to relieve the horse's back. The reins should be left long enough for the horse to balance himself. When the slope is very steep it is safer to get off and lead, but make sure that you walk beside the horse and never go in front, in case the horse stumbles.

In and around forests and woods, riders will also have to cope with low hanging branches. If they can't be avoided, riders will have to duck to avoid getting hit in the face. If riding in a group, keep a safe distance from the horse in

If the path is overgrown on both sides then it may be a tight squeeze. (Photo: Kite Houghton)

A rider will need to avoid low hanging branches by ducking.

A well-trained horse will walk calmly through water. (Photo: Kite Houghton)

front so that branches swinging back won't do any harm to the rider following.

Rivers and streams should only be crossed once a horse has become used to water. Horses that are scared or inexperienced in going through water can be a danger if they get upset or rear. Well-schooled horses trained through water should have no problems. If you need to ride through a stream, choose the flattest route through with the firmest possible footing. Before crossing, check that the water level is not too high and that the current is not too strong. Otherwise the horse can lose his footing and endanger himself and his rider.

If dogs running loose get out of control they can be dangerous to horse and rider.

Overcoming potential dangers safely

Unusual situations or events as well as fear-inducing objects demand a greater level of alertness as well as preventive action. Whether in fields or woods, a rider must be prepared to encounter others seeking peace and quiet and relaxation, whether these be walkers or mountain bikers, who not infrequently appear to understand nothing at all about horses. Because of this lack of knowledge, such people will often behave incorrectly and endanger riders. When out hacking, a rider needs to take this into account and avoid conflicts or accidents by taking appropriate measures such as slowing down, keeping a safe distance or avoiding other people totally. Extreme caution should be exercised where loose dogs are running around, as they may provoke a horse's natural instincts to flee from predators if the dog runs up from behind or decides to attack. Disobedient dogs need to be put on a leash as soon as possible, and this needs to be made clear to the dog's owner by shouting or hand signals. Further problems may be caused by other horses out at pasture or other grazing animals, and this should be prepared for by proceeding at a walk and keeping your distance. Animals running along the fence beside you, and the noises, movement and smells of farm animals or possibly exotic or other wild animals can cause a horse to take fright and shy or take off. To avoid any danger of infection or the possibility of injury through biting or kicking out, avoid letting the animals sniff each other.

Exercise proper care when riding next to cattle pasture.

To avoid getting into the line of fire, riders should also enquire of their local shoot or gamekeeper the dates of any shoots or stalking. Raised hides tend to be used in the evenings from the middle of May to the end of August. Foxhunting takes place primarily from October through to March. However it is not only hunters that can scare horses, but the wildlife too. You should be prepared for deer to cross your path, especially on the edges or woods or forests, and also in and out of crops, copses and set-aside. Usually horses will smell the other animals long before humans are aware of them so the rider can react accordingly. In addition certain wooded areas may be blocked off due to tree felling.

Tree felling and clearance can be life-threatening. Under no circumstances should you ride where there are warning signs of forestry work.

Objects such as a bench painted bright red suddenly appearing at the edge of a wood, or plastic sheeting left on a field by a forgetful farmer, or even a plastic bag in a hedge, can be scary even for an experienced horse. Your own calmness will have a calming effect on your horse. If he refuses to go forward, don't immediately try to make him go on, but allow him time to look at it, and if possible smell the apparently frightening object. If the horse can recognise the harmlessness of the object then he will usually go on past it.

Horses can get very suspicious of silage bales on the edge of fields or paths.

If it is getting dark, horse and rider are recognisable at best only in outline. At dusk the rider should be correctly equipped with reflective accessories, possibly also with a rider's light strapped onto the arm or leg.

If lightning is approaching, lakes and pools should be avoided.

Riding in bad weather and darkness

A rider's clothing should always suit the prevailing weather conditions and protect from the rain, wind and cold. The accessory market offers a range of weatherproof and protective clothing. Generally before going out riders should always check the weather forecast and any other signs that would indicate that there will be a change in conditions, so that they are prepared for any eventuality. If despite this you are surprised by a sudden thunderstorm, a safe place should immediately be sought out. Buildings with lightning conductors will offer best protection against lightening strike, as for example on farms or in an underpass. You will be relatively safe in low-lying areas such as sunken roads, valleys and within woods or forest, providing you are at least 150 metres from the edge of the cover. On the other hand hilltops, plateaus, open areas, isolated trees or shelters as well as power masts and water are very dangerous when there is lightning.

Violent storms, especially in autumn, that can blow objects through the air, or freezing rain in the winter months that can turn a path into an ice rink in a matter of minutes, can be dangerous for anyone riding out. You should never knowingly take a risk in this weather, instead return home immediately or wait until the weather front or storm has passed by.

In thick fog at dusk or in the dark, riders are almost impossible to see and are often only seen when it is too late.

This is especially dangerous when riding on the road. The Highway Code suggests that it is safer not to ride on the road at night or in poor visibility, but if you do, the horse should have reflective bands above the fetlock joints and the rider should carry a light that shows white to the front and red to the rear. If riding as part of a group, every rider and horse should wear the same reflective equipment. There is a wide variety of additional reflective clothing for both horse and rider, from breast-plates and tail wraps to hatbands and vests. This is for the rider's own safety as well as ensuring that all other road users can see the rider in good time. In addition, in poor visibility riders should try and use only wide and well-lit roads and paths.

A fluorescent vest and reflective leg wraps are clearly lit up in headlights.

Paddocks that border onto a road are ideal for horses to become accustomed to traffic.

particularly well suited for this purpose. Providing that the field is fenced securely, this will get a horse used to the noise and movement of traffic relatively quickly.

If you don't have this opportunity, you can also get your horse accustomed to traffic at home by leading him past vehicles and getting him used to motor and horn noises. Later you can practise by hacking out with another more experienced horse on quiet roads and next to railway lines.

Remember in addition that horses are particularly scared of large or loud vehicles. Hissing buses, roaring motorbikes, clattering lorries or the fluttering tarpaulin on a trailer are all real bogeymen for any inexperienced horse. To

Larger vehicles such as tractors can make already nervous horses more fearful.

Safe road riding

Particular care needs to be taken when riding in traffic. Any horse going out must be accustomed to vehicles and traffic noise at as early a stage as possible. As a rider you are obliged to know and obey the legislation contained in the Road Traffic Acts and the rules contained in the Highway Code. In addition you should also follow precautionary measures for the sake of your own safety. Horses that are unsafe in traffic are at high risk of causing accidents. Training a horse for traffic should be begun as early as possible. Grazing that is situated close to busy roads or next to railway lines is

*Getting a horse used to road markings is part
of a horse's education in traffic.*

avoid endangering the horse and all other road
users unnecessarily, it may be better to get off
and lead your horse until he has lost his fear.

Some horses also shy at the white road
markings. While one will view the markings as
jumps and jump over them, another will refuse
to walk over them. Some horses also refuse to
walk over manhole covers and make a wide
berth of them. In traffic such unexpected behaviour can be dangerous. You should therefore
make sure that your horse has already encoun-
tered such things in a safe place and is accustomed to them.

Riders and the law

The same laws and rules of the road apply to
horse riders as to other road users driving vehicles. Road signs and traffic lights apply to riders
as much as they do to other road users. For
example a rider must stop at a red light or, at an
intersection, give way as required. Footpaths
and cycle tracks should not be used by riders.

Horses are viewed as slow-moving vehicles
in the Highway Code and should always be ridden on the left. Small groups should ride in single file, larger groups should never ride more
than two abreast and where there are large

Always ride on the left-hand side of the road.

Before changing direction always give an appropriate hand signal.

groups, should be put into groups of six pairs with a distance between groups of at least 25 metres. Where the road narrows or when approaching a bend, always ride in single file. Inexperienced horses should always go on the inside and as far to the left as possible.

Before riding off or turning, a rider must look both to the front and behind him and give a clear arm signal. If a rider sees an obstacle such as a parked car that needs to be ridden around, then he will need to signal in advance and navigate around the obstacle leaving plenty of room.

If as a rider you need to cross the road, then this needs to be indicated to the stream of traffic as well. Single or pairs of riders should wait at the side of the road until there is a gap in the traffic and then cross quickly. Larger groups of riders should cross in pairs. On busier roads it may be necessary to stop the traffic in both directions. The first two riders should position themselves in the middle of the road to the right and left of the group and ask the traffic to stop with arm signals.

According to the law, horses should only be introduced to traffic when they are accompanied by a suitably experienced person. This means the person must be able to control the ridden or led horse. The horse must be tacked up to enable the person to exert the necessary control. You may need to check what your insurance company will regard as suitable tack. You should always lead a horse on the extreme left of the carriageway. If more than one horse is being led, the horses must be tied to each other (up to four horses); however, for reasons of safety never more than one horse should be led at a time.

Riders should only cross the road when there is a gap in the traffic.

Horses should be led on the left-hand side of the road.

In the case of railway lines and level crossings, riders still need to follow the legal requirements for traffic. Crossing railway lines at any place other than a proper crossing is forbidden, apart for the fact that it would be very dangerous. Just like other traffic, riders should cross train tracks at level crossings. Where there are barriers on the crossing, stay at a safe distance from the traffic and the barrier, and only proceed when all the other traffic has crossed. Take particular care at crossings where there are no barriers. Don't rely solely on the signals and before crossing check that the tracks are clear.

For their own safety riders should behave with caution and ride defensively in all types of traffic. Always expect others to behave unexpectedly. Vehicles that are travelling either too fast or too close to horses should be asked to slow down or keep their distance through the use of hand signals.

The law also applies to riders: only ever cross railways lines at a proper crossing point.

ses. For this reason, when starting out always lead a horse over a bridge, preferably in the company of another more experienced horse.

When riding through underpasses you have the opposite situation, because here the traffic appears to be clattering over the horse's head. In addition the horse may find the changing light conditions, from light to dark, and the echoing sounds in such a tunnel-like structure, particularly spooky. The first few times it is again best to lead and take company.

It is sometimes necessary to ride through built-up areas. You should always reckon with situations that will startle a horse, such as a window suddenly being opened, a newspaper being blown along the ground or a barking dog rushing

Riding over bridges and through underpasses and built-up areas

When available, use bridges or underpasses wherever possible to cross roads or railway tracks. A prerequisite though is that they are also closed for use to all other traffic, otherwise in an emergency you will have no escape route and that could be disastrous. Horses still need to get used to crossing bridges. Unusual surroundings, the drop below and the traffic flowing apparently under his hooves can be scary for many hor-

Underpasses are a safe alternative to crossing roads or tracks.

*Road works and building sites should be
carefully skirted around.*

up to a gate. For this reason it may be safer and
less nerve-wracking to go by foot. Building sites
can be particularly dangerous for horse and rider,
and should be given plenty of distance. Many
dangers can lurk around building sites. Noisy
machines, rattling scaffolding or nails and wire
that may lie to the side of the site are only a few
of these. If you can't avoid them, then it can be
safer to get off and lead your horse past, either
on the opposite side of the road or with the horse
held at arm's length, as this can help keep the
horse at a distance if he does get startled.

Problem horses as a safety risk

Spooky, stubborn or flighty horses can put their riders in very difficult situations when out hacking. What are the causes for such difficulties and how can you correct this behaviour?

In a gallop horses will often egg each other on.

Most frequent problems

One very frequent problem is the tendency to shy. Over-anxious horses will start at the slightest thing, even at their own shadow. Jumping to one side or rearing, which is often connected with this, can put a rider into a very nasty position. Not a few horses will also bolt after shying at something, as they try to get to safety through flight. If the horse panics and blindly races off, he won't let himself be stopped and the rider is relatively powerless to do anything. Horses that are forward-moving types may also get out of control if they lean on the reins or go behind the bit and thus can avoid any of the usual aids.

Horses that won't be ridden with others will be a risk in group rides.

Another unpleasant characteristic is napping. A nappy horse is one that won't or only with a great deal of persuasion allows himself to be ridden away from other horses or home. This can be hazardous for the rider if the horse suddenly turns around and tries to take off back to home. Horses that can't be ridden in a group can also endanger themselves and other riders. Some won't be ridden at the back of a group

A hefty buck may unseat the rider and put him in danger.

Confined movement is often responsible for over-reactions when the horse is ridden out.

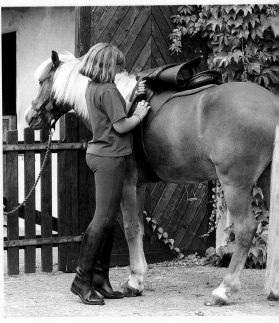

A poorly fitted saddle or one that is girthed up too quickly can cause problems.

and will always be trying to overtake the others and get to the front. Others refuse to go at the front, will try to veer off to the side or will refuse to go forwards at all.

Another problem that should not be underestimated is constant stumbling. Horses that lose their footing at the slightest unevenness will be more likely to stumble. If they lose their balance and can't catch themselves then they may fall and in the worst scenario drop their rider underneath themselves. Many, especially more lively horses, may also tend to buck when going into canter, though this is usually harmless, Repeated bucking with the aim of ridding themselves of their rider by dropping the head down and rounding the back up can be more dangerous.

Causes of behavioural problems

Vices such as rearing or bucking are not inborn problems but instead are caused by mistakes made either in the way horses are kept and handled, as a result of training or by the way they are ridden. You need to honestly and self-critically explore what problems your horse may have and what causes the discomfort or even pain that may result in disobedience.

Inactivity as a result of continuous stabling can often lead to bad habits such as rushing, bolting and bucking, and is often seen in connection with too much hard feed.

Napping and easily frightened horses are usually uncertain and fearful animals with little self-confidence and little trust in people. If such a horse then gets a similarly fearful rider, the whole problem is just worsened. Mistakes in training such as breaking in too early or by an inexperienced rider can be the reason for a horse trying to get rid of his rider by rearing or bucking. Apart from bad experiences, omissions during the basic training and serious riding mistakes are to blame for many bad habits.

Permanently asking too much of a horse or at the other end of the scale, over-indulgence or inconsistencies, can lead to disobedience. Pulling or rushing is encouraged by always cantering at the same spot on a ride, or by allowing the horse to determine his own pace. Holding the reins too short can increase nervousness and a tendency to shy and trying to push on while holding back in an attempt to collect a horse results not infrequently in rearing.

Unsuitable tack, or tack that is too harsh, as well as an ill-fitting saddle that makes a horse uncomfortable or even causes pain, are further possible causes for behaviour such as rearing, bucking or bolting. As a result of a poorly fitting saddle, or girthing up too quickly, a horse may become "cold backed" and become known as a bucker.

Excessive stumbling is frequently a sign that a trip to the farrier is overdue or that the toes of the shoes are too long. But conformation faults, illnesses affecting a horse's limbs or spine, tension in the back as a result of saddle pressure or trouble in the forehand, can all result in a tendency to stumble.

Finally a wide range of illnesses and physical problems that cause pain and discomfort can all be responsible for causing problems in horses. The most immediate to consider are always those linked to the back or teeth, muscular inflammations, heart and lung infections, allergies as well as problems or changes to the limbs and hooves.

Getting difficult horses under control

First it is necessary to look for the cause of a problem and consider how and whether it can be alleviated or got rid of. To do this you need to examine and check the horse's exterior, his state of health and condition, his shoeing and the state of his feet and the equipment used with the horse. Furthermore any mistakes in the way the horse is kept must be ruled out. Changing to a more natural

Riding over small branches increases a horse's surefootedness.

management system, for example from being stabled 23 hours a day to being turned out, can often be the quickest solution for bad behaviour.

Excited horses that tend to pulling or jogging can be brought under control by a long-term programme of deliberately walking them out, followed by frequent changes of pace. Horses that rear out of pure naughtiness should be ridden strongly forward on a loose rein.

In many cases however it is recommended that such problem horses be started again from scratch so that any mistakes in their original training can be ironed out, or anything that was missed out can be done. For horses that don't like being ridden as part of a group, the reason usually lies in some omission in their early training. Group riding should be practised at home, with horses learning the basic rules such as keeping a distance, riding alongside others and learning to change the position in the group.

Horses that go more on the forehand, resulting in frequent stumbling, have usually not been taught to use their back properly and come through from behind with their quarters underneath them. Through gymnastic exercises a horse's elasticity and submissiveness can be increased by, for example, riding up hills, riding small circles around trees and riding serpentines through rows of trees. In addition the attentiveness of horses prone to stumbling can be increased by riding over poles or cavalettis.

In the case of nappy horses or those who shy more than most, trust will need to be built up. Use short walks on foot to build up trust between rider and horse. Later and once the horse is out of ear-shot and sight of the rest of the herd or stable mates, mount and ride on further, gradually lengthening the ride. Horses with a greater than normal tendency to shy can be put through a special programme of groundwork, which will reduce levels of fear gradually. The horse then learns to cope with apparently scary objects and situations instead of fleeing from them.

Such corrective programmes need to be designed on an individual basis and followed step by step. Rushing or trying strong bits and force are counterproductive and have no place in the process at all.

The desired result will be based on a foundation of four pillars: trust, patience, consistency and practice. A rider has to ask herself whether she is up to the task. Any lack of knowledge or riding experience will need to be filled in or refreshed. If you feel overwhelmed by the task of overcoming a problem then go to an expert instead. Under no circumstances should you hack out on a horse that you know to be difficult, but instead you should concentrate on working at home and avoid any situation that may cause a problem until you know that you have it under control.

Until a horse, that was previously prone to shying, can accept a rider with an umbrella, it requires a carefully structured anti-shying training programme.